SPECT─

HANGING

BASKETS

JOHN FELTWELL

SPECTACULAR
HANGING
BASKETS

CASSELL

Cassell Publishers Ltd

Wellington House, 125 Strand

London WC2R 0BB

Text copyright © John Feltwell 1997

Photographs copyright © Garden Matters/John Feltwell 1997

First published 1997

British Library Cataloguing in Publication Data

A Catalogue record for this book is available from the British Library

ISBN 0-304-34614-4

Distributed in the United States by

Sterling Publishing Co. Inc.,

387 Park Avenue South, New York, NY 10016-8810

Edited by Caroline Ball

Printed and bound in Spain

Contents

INTRODUCTION

Baskets enhance any garden, enlivening a dull corner, colouring a bare wall, displaying a prize specimen – many pendulous or trailing plants can only be fully appreciated when seen from below. And they can fulfil horticultural fantasies: cottage gardeners can indulge a secret passion for lush jungles; budding designers can experiment with innovative, even bizarre, ideas; green fingers without a garden to tend can create a green world in a basket.

Hanging baskets can be one of the most rewarding forms of gardening – or one of the most frustrating. How often our anticipation of a hanging garden to equal Babylon's has turned to disappointment as our flowery vision wilts and runs to seed, colours clash instead of harmonizing or a promising plant turns out to be a real non-performer! Because of this, baskets are all too often planted up to the same tried and tested formula, sacrificing creativity and daring. But, as the suggestions and plantings in this book show, imagination can yield spectacular results.

'Tinkerbell', a fine white fuchsia, makes a splendid basket display throughout the summer and autumn.

ACHIEVING THE SPECTACULAR

How do you transform an ordinary basket into a truly spectacular one? To catch the eye, any basket plants must be really bursting with health and married successfully with their container and surroundings, but a little lateral thinking can help create something special.

The element of surprise can often work. Just about anything, within reason, can be put into a hanging basket, and that includes shrubs and trees. Of course, dwarf varieties are most suitable, as well as young or bonsai specimens. A young camellia can be used effectively for the glossiness of its young leaves and that old Christmas favourite, the poinsettia, gains new dramatic interest when treated as a basket plant (see page 117).

Here, the startling trumpet of a rich pink *Hibiscus rosa-sinensis* not only makes one look twice but lends style to the more familiar flowers which frame it. Hibiscus are normally grown as large standards or stout shrubs in the flower border, but dwarf stock can be encouraged to perform in rather more restricted spaces with pleasing results. Unlike many reduced forms, dwarf hibiscus do not have correspondingly small flowers. Pairing the exotic hibiscus with the froth of alyssum (*Lobularia maritima*) is eye-catching, but choosing such a deep-coloured lobelia (this is *Lobelia erinus* 'Blue Pearl') ensures that the effect is not unbalanced.

Hibiscus rosa-sinensis framed by lobelia and alyssum.

Tradescantia 'Tahiti Bridal Veil'.

Try something new so that your baskets become a focus of interest and speculation. Many unusual plants are well suited to basket life and, singled out as a feature, can be shown off to full advantage. The ethereal quality of *Tradescantia* 'Tahiti Bridal Veil' would surely not be so apparent in a pot. *Russelia equisetiformis* AGM, the coral plant or fountain bush, is an uncommon tender shrub which originates from Cuba and Central America where its flowers are naturally attractive to humming-birds and insects. It prefers a lot of warmth and in

Russelia equisetiformis AGM, the coral plant or fountain bush.

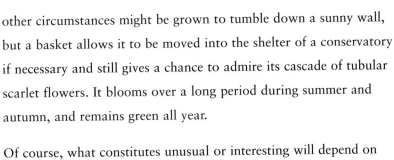

other circumstances might be grown to tumble down a sunny wall, but a basket allows it to be moved into the shelter of a conservatory if necessary and still gives a chance to admire its cascade of tubular scarlet flowers. It blooms over a long period during summer and autumn, and remains green all year.

Of course, what constitutes unusual or interesting will depend on your point of view and geography: the cherished portulacas and gazanias of temperate gardens are as prolific as weeds in their native South Africa. Garden centres now offer such a superb range of tropical and sub-tropical plants, often at reasonable prices, that a problem can be choice, not lack of choice. The final chapter in this book shows many more possibilities.

Simplicity is often the best trick of all. This can be more difficult to achieve with a mixed planting (although the exotic basket on page 125 is a admirable example of a mixed planting of almost Japanese simplicity), so the most striking results are usually attained by focusing on a single species or cultivar. The tuberous begonia opposite makes a staggering display, with nothing to dilute the impact of those huge fluffy blossoms. Indeed, any accompanying plants here might have served as an unnecessary distraction rather than an enhancement of the overall effect. In a successful mixed basket, the whole should amount to more than the sum of the parts, but in a solo act like this, restraint always pays off.

Large apricot tuberous begonia.

A ball of pink impatiens: easy yet full of impact.

Campanulas come in many forms, many of which grow on vertical surfaces and loose ground in the wild, so it is natural to give these plants the opportunity to stretch out and cascade over the side of a basket. Their charm is enhanced by the restraint of this planting in a wicker basket.

To succeed in this sort of display plants have to be at their very best, as any shortcomings cannot be disguised – the impact of the impatiens above would be completely lost if it were not such a floriferous ball of health. Popularly known as Busy Lizzies, impatiens grow fast to put on a marvellous display all summer, and do not require full sun. They come in a pretty palette of colours (see page 54).

Wicker basket with a simple planting of campanulas.

Petunias, lobelia and verbena in a harmony of mauves.

Abundance is probably the most obvious way of creating impact, but an extremely effective one. This stunner (left) is nothing more than a swag of petunias leavened with verbena and lobelia, but what a show to be proud of! Tuberous begonias will tend to dominate any basket, but here (right) the begonia's apricot frills would seem less exuberant without the contrast of the little red rose and purple haze of lobelia, and (below) the delicate blue bush violets (*Browallia speciosa*) serve to heighten the jewel-like brilliance of the beautiful begonias.

Red, yellow and apricot begonias acccompanied by a delicate bush violet.

Opposite: Large apricot tuberous begonia mixed with lobelia.

Above: a bold colour scheme built around African marigolds and scarlet petunias.
Right: so similar, and yet not nearly so successful.

Combinations of colour are so important to the success of hanging baskets. It is very easy to play safe and go for a one-colour arrangement, or to limit the palette to harmonious pastels. Bold use of colour can be sensational – or a sensational flop – and it is worth learning a little about how hues and shades affect one another. Compare these two, very similar baskets: each has used the sunny yellow of African marigolds (*Tagetes erecta*) to catch the eye, with white alyssum and pale lobelia to lighten the effect. A pretty but predictable way to have completed the picture would have been with white petunias or lots more foliage. The choice of pink petunias (below) is certainly more audacious but not a happy partnership – it takes the strength of scarlet (left) to succeed. Where the brilliant red makes the marigolds glow, the pink simply makes them brassy. However, one of the beauties of hanging baskets is that their small scale encourages experimentation which we might baulk at in the open garden.

WHICH PLANTS?

The choice of plants for hanging baskets is often bewildering, as any trip round a garden centre will tell. Every year new cultivars are developed, in some cases looking far removed from the parents or stock they were developed from. Fuchsias, for example, seem to be getting more exciting with every season, with larger trusses of flowers and ever more adventurous colours. A similar boom is going on in other basket favourites, as variegated impatiens, cascade carnations and bi-coloured petunias are introduced on to the market. A helpful guide is to look for plants marked AGM (Award of Garden Merit), given by the Royal Horticultural Society to plants of outstanding garden excellence.

This is Mayeda's Nursery in Orange County, California: the clouds of colour from hanging begonias, fuchsias, impatiens and ferns, with the floor carpeted with further floral delights, demonstrate the variety available in just a few types of plant. The whole area is covered in shade cloth which protects the flowers and foliage from the burning effect of direct sunlight, and the plants are well watered at least twice a day.

Mayeda's Nursery, southern California.

Fast making their mark are previously unconsidered tender perennials: *Scaevola*, *Bacopa*, *Felicia* and a host of others have all become hugely popular in recent years and many are proving great hanging basket plants. Part of the fun of gardening is using some of these new species with old favourites.

Scaevola aemula, the beach naupaka or blue fan.

A beautiful plant from the beaches of Australia, *Scaevola* is referred to more by its Latin name than by its other more descriptive name of beach naupaka. These are tough plants, which you might expect from species which are often buffeted by wind and salt spray. Their sprawling habit, which sends their thick stems through drifts of sand, is usefully employed in hanging baskets for lateral growth. Its curious five-lobed flowers appear in profusion the length of the fleshy stems. Attractive grown by itself, it also mixes well with other, more traditonal basket plants and lasts well into the first frosts.

Look out, too, for completely new varieties. Giving the distinct impression of being a pendulous variety of pink or carnation, this is in fact a double variety of a European seaside plant, *Silene maritima* (syn. *uniflora*) or sea campion: this is 'Maiden's Tears'. In cultivation it has lost all similarity to its original form which has five delicate petals and a much smaller habit – this one is a new-comer with a spectacular difference.

Silene maritima 'Maiden's Tears'.

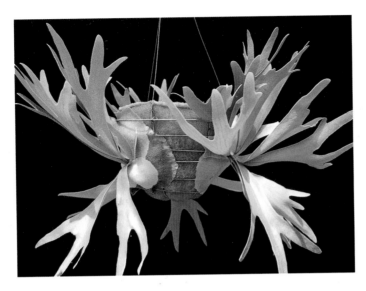

A pair of stag's horn ferns, *Platycerium bifurcatum* (= *alcicorne*) AGM.

Just like hemlines and ties, there are fashions in gardening and a certain type of plant or colour scheme will be sought after one year and dismissed scornfully the next. This does not mean you have to follow fashion, but it does have an effect on the availability of plants: market forces at play. However, a plant does not have to be labelled 'for hanging baskets' to make a good basket plant. Think laterally. In the wild, epiphytic plants and air plants spend their lives high up in the forest canopy clinging on to other plants; a hanging basket provides a not dissimilar habitat and an excellent way of displaying these tree-dwellers.

Ferns do not readily spring to mind for baskets as often as they should, yet they offer spectacular displays. The filigree effect of the foliage of many ferns and the strap-like nature of others, the subtle variations in green and their graceful arching nature provide a wide variety of features for any gardener with baskets in mind. Ferns have two other useful attributes: they are perennial and most thrive in poor light levels.

Look for any plants which are naturally pendulous, or have a tendency to climb as these will usually trail without support. But even more upright varieties can be reshaped by careful training or judicious pruning. The truth about hanging baskets is that you can put anything in them, from ferns, wild flowers, herbs and house plants to herbaceous perennials and shrubs or even mini-trees.

TYPES OF BASKET

Baskets at garden centres come in a few standard forms, but do not let that cramp your style. Wire or wooden lathe baskets are useful and adaptable, but in fact any container can be hoisted up and suspended on wire or chains – a hollowed-out section of tree trunk suspended from a branch can look magnificent.

Wire and plastic baskets are designed to be hidden by strong-growing plants, but many wooden, wicker and other containers are attractive enough to form part of the overall design.

Here is a 'hanging basket' with a difference: a slice of tree trunk which can be secured to a post or hung in free space. Anchored to it is a stag's horn fern, *Platycerium superbum* (= *grande*), clearly displaying its sucker-like fronds over the surface of the wood. Suspended like this in the sunshine, the net-like veins in the 'antlers' are effectively revealed.

Platycerium superbum (= *grande*).

The closely planted small flowers of petunias, alyssum, African marigolds and lobelia (above) grow through mesh lined with sphagnum moss and pieces of gnarled wood to give this patio a more rustic touch.

The woven basket on the right makes a statement, containing a tight collection of African marigolds, petunias, salvias, *Begonia semperflorens* and various pinks (*Dianthus spp.*).

The petunia above with the raspberry ripple stripes is 'Frenzy Red Star'.

The white of the wicker basket, left, complements the ice cream tones of these petunias. In a few weeks the flowers and foliage will have filled out to cover the inner pot but without obscuring the basket (see page 46).

PRACTICALITIES

When first planted, baskets will look a little sparse, but with regular feeding and, if necessary, pinching out, the plants will very quickly establish themselves. Having achieved a spectacular display it is always important to keep baskets in good health. Slow-release fertilizers, water-retaining gels, special long-necked watering cans and sprays and automatic drip irrigation can all help make the regular watering and feeding regime less arduous, but baskets will still need a daily check: dead blooms, diseases and pests may play havoc even with a masterpiece.

In an exposed position, baskets can all too soon look windswept and dry out beyond recall. If possible, plant up more baskets than are needed – these stand-ins can then replace vulnerable baskets to give them a respite and time to recover. They can also serve to ring the changes as the season progresses. *Kalanchoes* make good plants for baskets, being relatively slow-growing, drought tolerant and attractive all year round, but deadheading will improve the overall appearance of this *Kalanchoe pumila* AGM (left) from Madagascar enormously.

Right: a newly planted half-basket.

Left: a floriferous kalanchoe.

1   Place the liner in the basket.

2   Open the wires to allow room for the plants.

3   Cut planting holes in the liner with scissors.

4   Insert a plant into each prepared hole.

5   Fill the basket with damp, soilless compost.

6   Add a final plant on top and water in well.

HOW TO MAKE A SIMPLE HANGING BASKET

The most popular form of hanging basket is the wire hemisphere – inexpensive,
light and designed for the purpose. Baskets like this should be planted all round
(this one has four impatiens around the sides and one on top), so the final effect is
a suspended ball of flowers, hiding the basket from view.

SETTING

Selecting the right plants or combination of plants, planting and caring for them is not the end of the story. The impact a basket can make is greatly influenced by its surroundings. Sometimes, to be effective, a basket needs a lone, prominent position where it can be viewed from all sides without a distracting background. Others only come into their own as an integral part of an arrangement, such as around a front door or steps, partnering window boxes, pots and containers. We are used to seeing baskets hanging beside doors or adorning walls or pergolas, but try them out in other places: swinging from mature trees, freestanding in a courtyard, suspended in a stairwell – and indoors, too, in a conservatory or any room with sufficient light.

Placing colour can be important. Silvery, white or pale green can act like a shaft of sunlight in a dark corner or bring a sense of calm to a quiet spot. A strategically placed basket can bring a brilliant highlight to a dull area or extend the interest of an out-of-season tree. A series of matching hanging baskets gives a sense of continuity or can draw the eye along a wall or walk. Very pendulous plants, similarly, can emphasize verticality or point the way, perhaps to a specific plant or garden feature below.

The overall effect in the scene opposite is very restful, the plants carefully chosen to complement the white conservatory, a small statue and the natural wood furniture. The baskets contain *Helichrysum petiolare* AGM, pale pink roses, white *Lychnis coronaria* and the aromatic foliage of *Santolina chamaecyparissus* AGM.

Silver and greens in a Sussex courtyard.

In contrast with the previous scene, this suspended log swinging from the bough of an oak in Mississippi speaks of the sultry tropics. Decorated with the dark leaves of *Neoregelia* bromeliads and white impatiens, it immediately attracts attention, a splash of vibrant colour among the greenery. Along the bough is a natural covering of resurrection fern (*Polypodium polypodioides*), so named because its withered brown fronds suddenly spring to rich green after rain.

Nasturtiums (*Tropaeolum majus*) are cheap and easy to grow and can quickly provide a splash of colour wherever it is needed. Being annuals, they come and go in a season, but this can be an advantage when experimenting with bold colour combinations. Many of the climbing forms can be encouraged to trail from a basket. Look for a single colour variety such as this, rather than a mixed packet of seed, if you want more control over the effect. As a bonus, their attractive and distinctively rounded leaves are edible as, indeed, are the flowers.

Above: Climbing nasturtiums are ideal for tumbling, too.
Opposite: A bough for a basket of sub-tropical splendour.

Because they are so portable, baskets do not need to stay in the same place all year, or even all season. A basket of miniature bulbs and ivy planted up to bring a promise of spring to a front porch can be replaced by a summer display which has been waiting in the wings for the last frosts. The spring basket could be replanted, perhaps with a different colour scheme to ring the changes half way through the summer, or to be usefully employed elsewhere in the garden. A few baskets are a quick and satisfying way to bring life and colour to a blossom tree drab after its period of beauty, the raw corners of a new house, a pergola or archway still waiting for its clothing of climbers . . .

the possibilities are endless.

Baskets can decorate the inside of the house as well, filled either with permanent house plants, or as a temporary shelter for tender specimens. This unusual ivy-leaved trailing violet from Australia, *Viola hederacea* (right), is quite unlike its many clump-forming relatives; it deserves to have attention drawn to it. In warm weather it can be hung outside but needs to be taken in during any cooler periods.

Left: adaptable impatiens bring colour to a bare pergola.

Right: *Viola hederacea.*

Once you begin to look at plants for their potential in baskets, horizons are suddenly broadened. Hanging baskets will undoubtedly always be, first and foremost, part of the summer garden; but create a bit of instant winter magic with primulas or early bulbs; seek out small shrubs to provide year-round interest; see if some of your house plants might not actually be happier and better displayed in a basket. Even cut flowers make a stupendous temporary display.

Cut flowers in a willow basket at Hampton Court Flower Show.

Early primulas and an ornamental cabbage (*Brassica* sp.) form the basis of a basket which can be put together in minutes and cheer up the dullest winter.

PETUNIAS AND PALS

Petunias, impatiens (Busy Lizzies) and lobelia are some of the stalwarts of hanging baskets. When aiming for the spectacular it is easy to pass them over in favour of newcomers with more street cred, but these old troopers have remained favourites for the very sound reasons that they can be counted on to give a tremendous show and are inexpensive enough to allow you to splash out on a really generous display.

Petunias are extremely floriferous over a long season and are available in almost every shade imaginable in the pink-blue spectrum, from velvety magenta to ice blue. The petunia is a member of the potato family and the garden varieties originate from hybrids of a native of the warmer parts of Latin America. Hybridisation between the two basic sorts of petunias – the small-flowered Multifloras and the larger-flowered Grandifloras – has produced a range of cultivars, some of them marketed under the Celebrity and Mirage series. Double forms are an interesting variation and the recent surfinia hybrids introduced flowers with attractive veining (see page 46).

This towering display shows how a little ingenuity can transform everyday basket plants into a spectacle, but it will need a lot of watering to keep it going all summer.

Impatiens are the mainstay of so many hanging baskets the world over. Their qualities lie in their great range of colour, the way that each plant becomes covered with flowers, their fast growth rate, ease of propagation, and their tolerance of low light levels. Throughout much of North America, particularly down the eastern seaboard where a lot of gardening takes place beneath the shade of trees, impatiens are invaluable, while in the high humidity of the deep south, they grow to huge proportions, with stems as thick as fingers. In Britain the impatiens is a more delicate creature, much favoured as a house plant, but it also provides invaluable colour in baskets since it will thrive in a dull, wet summer.

The same properties of floriferous fast growth, easy propagation and innumerable colour variations in the scarlet-pink-mauve-white spectrum are shared by those other reliable stalwarts, pelargoniums. However, where impatiens are unbeatable in the shade, perlargoniums prefer full sun and are usefully drought-resistant.

The African marigold, *Tagetes erecta*, is not, confusingly, from Africa, but central America. It is usually seen contributing its tightly knit heads of golden petals and feathery foliage to beds and borders, but African marigolds and their smaller relations, the French marigolds (*Tagetes patula*), make attractive and versatile plants for hanging baskets. They grow easily from seed and hybridisation has generated several different forms, some with exceedingly large heads, but all within the yellow/orange/mahogany range. The true marigolds, deriving from *Calendula officinalis*, can be used in baskets too. They have been used medicinally for thousands of years and also have yellow flowers, but have less elegant and undivided leaves.

Trailing plants are always a particularly effective element in a basket, and lobelias are a firm favourite. Despite their fragile appearance, small clumps of lobelia (*Lobelia erinus*) will soon bush up and send out long delicate strings of flowers and their shades of blue and white look good in almost any colour scheme. Contributing to the palette an exciting range of magenta, shocking pink and scarlet as well as white and rich purple, are the verbenas, whose long stems skitter over the sand in

Magenta petunias combined with double pink pelargonium in a richly coloured display.

their parched native habitat. Similar in habit, but very different in appearance, are the fleshy *Scaevola* (see page 23). Other newer introductions which have quickly proved their worth and can be seen on the following pages include the Swan River daisies (*Brachycome iberidifolia)*, *Bidens* (*B. ferulifolia* AGM) and the prolific *Sutera cordata*, usually labelled *Bacopa*.

The gamut of petunia shades (above) offset by a white wicker basket.

New forms of trailing petunias (right) made an entrance on to the gardening scene in 1994 with their massive cascades of flowers, the colours suffused with light and dark markings. They were hybridised in Japan, exported to Holland and thus made their way to Britain, and quickly became very popular in hanging baskets. Unfortunately, the strain became highly susceptible to a serious infection in 1995, which wiped out many stocks. Trailing petunias are propagated by cuttings, and therein lies the problem, since the same material is used repeatedly for raising stock. Other petunia varieties are raised from seed which gives them greater resistance.

Balance is difficult to maintain throughout the season: although the pink petunia in this large basket is growing well it has been banished to the bottom of the basket by the exuberance of the trailing lobelia.

The strong upright stems of these pink and white mandevillas arrange themselves very elegantly around an African marigold, white petunias and a yellow helichrysum to make a very full hanging basket.

A single lobelia flower is insignificant, but the effect *en masse* is strong enough to present
the perfect complement (above) to the bright yellow chrysanthemum flowers in what should
prove a long-lasting display. Opposite, lobelia billows in an airy cloud of white-eyed rubies.

What a display pelargoniums put on! They perform best in places where there is a long hot summer, which is usually denied in such places as Britain, but in other parts of the world, notably eastern Europe and the northern Mediterranean countries, hanging baskets made up entirely of pelargoniums are a common sight. Their main colour is red, sometimes a very vibrant red, which is especially striking when grown *en masse* in baskets or ranks of window boxes. Pelargoniums are still popularly known as geraniums, which actually describes another genus altogether, the hardy cranesbills. There is an enormous variety of pelargoniums, and a constant introduction of exciting new hybrids, many of which have a trailing nature, and it is these which are most popular with hanging basket enthusiasts.

Here are ivy-leaved pelargoniums, aptly named after their attractive leaves, one with single flowers (left), the other with double. If moved into a conservatory or greenhouse before the frosts, they can be kept over the winter, to produce their colourful performance from year to year.

In shady conditions few plants can match impatiens for colour. This pretty ball (left) illustrates the gamut of shades available, from scarlet and rich coral to pale blush pink and white.

The salmon-coloured impatiens below is one of several varieties with the additional attraction of pretty gold-veined leaves.

This huge ball of white flowers is produced by a sprawling plant from South Africa called *Sutera cordata* (syn. *Bacopa cordata*), of which there are about 140 *Bacopa* species known; many are much larger and taller than this attractive one. The tiny flowers of this compact form, called 'Snowflake', each have five petals enclosing a small yellow tube. *Sutera* is a member of the figwort family, many of which grow by water, so in order to keep this sutera so good-looking a daily dunking in water, or spraying, would be ideal. *Sutera* makes a stunning display by itself but mixes well with other plants and can be propagated by seed or by cuttings.

Diascias are well known as distinguished guests in the rock garden and have an enviable range of delicately patterned flowers. There are few small plants that have such an attractive structure and arrangement of flowers. The plants are generally low-growing, very prolific in flower and sometimes have a sprawling nature, although others are more upright. In a hanging basket they grow well, mostly upwards and outwards, rather than down and trailing. This one is *Diascia vigilis* AGM.

This effervescent brachycome is so covered with blooms that it is difficult to see it is making up a huge hanging basket ball. Easily grown from seeds, this member of the aster family produces a mass of flowers during the summer, making for a spectacular display ideal for hanging baskets. The yellow-centred daisy flowers are similar to those of another tender perennial popular for containers, *Felicia amelloides*, but are a little more feathery. Brachycomes are native mostly to Australia and New Zealand and there is a number of distinct species, such as the Swan River daisy (*B. iberidifolia*), and a few cultivars – 'Lemon Drops', 'Blue Star' and 'Pink Mist' suggest the colour range available.

If planning a stunning display in yellow, there is little to outshine *Bidens ferulifolia* AGM. Prolific in terms of flowers and with a light, much-divided structure, the effect of *Bidens* in a basket is quite magnificent. Here it is mixed effectively with a white chrysanthemum. *Bidens* is allied to the *Cosmos* family – and looks similar to some of these species in colour and size – as well as to *Coreopsis*, which, like *Bidens*, is also known confusingly as tickseed. *Bidens* also goes under the common names of bur marigold and beggar-ticks.

Verbenas are a popular choice in hanging baskets for their huge variety of colour, from bright reds, pinks, purple to lavender and white. Sometimes called vervains, they represent a large group of some 200 species native to South America and the warmer parts of North America – in the foothills of California they contribute to the floral beauty of the countryside following a generous period of rain. In the wild they live in dry sunny spots and their prostrate form is well suited to scrabbling over sandy soils. This habit gives them a great advantage in hanging baskets, in which their floriferous long stems cascade over the rim. Verbenas are easy to propagate from seed: they are quick to germinate and soon grow to flowering size.

White and lavender trailing lobelia complete a pretty picture in this arrangement, right, with fuchsias, petunias, pelargoniums and wax begonias. The colours highlight the white weather boarding behind, typical of many buildings in Kent.

Below, a dark-leaved variety of wax begonia (*Begonia semperflorens*), red petunia, white alyssum and deep purple lobelia combine to make an effective display in a simple Japanese-style wooden basket.

Incorporating gnarled pieces of old wood within the framework of a basket lined with sphagnum moss gives an agreeably rustic look from which a mêlée of flowers can look out. This basket contains palest pink salvia, wax begonias, pelargoniums, African marigolds, white petunias and alyssum and purple lobelia.

This tastefully decorated cottage (opposite) uses every means available, it seems, to display flowers and foliage to their best advantage, including conventional hanging baskets, window boxes and, rather more unusually, a porch roof box!

FUCHSIAS AND BEGONIAS

Gardeners would be stuck without fuchsias. They contribute striking reds, whites and purples to the garden, lasting well into the autumn and they can be used in beds, borders and containers of all sorts. Their great flare, however, seems to be as subjects in hanging baskets, and they often need no other plants with them to make a visual impact.

Not all fuchsias are suitable for hanging baskets but enough of the hundreds of varieties available are, and many firm favourites have been established, with excellent new cultivars coming along all the time. Those which are by nature trailing are eminently suited to baskets, and although many are tender and have to be brought in or sheltered during the winter, some originate in the wild and windy parts of South America and have surprisingly hardy characteristics.

Fuchsias do best in a reasonably humid atmosphere and appreciate some shade – many of the white-flowered varieties will turn quite pink in full sun. They reach their peak when the height of summer has past and, given the benefit of regular

'Swingtime' AGM, a very distinctive fuchsia with glossy red sepals enclosing a great frill of wavy white petals: a very popular choice for hanging baskets.

watering and feeding, will continue
to give of their best all through the
autumn when many other basket
plants have wilted or gone to seed.
Just occasionally, fuchsias will set
fruit and these juicy morsels are,
in fact, edible.

Fuchsias can be overwintered
somewhere frost free (they will
usually lose their leaves) for extra-
large specimens the following year,
but cuttings that are taken in the
summer will root quickly and are
an easy way of providing a new
generation of plants.

The narrow sepals of the aptly named
'Red Spider' arch outwards to give the
effect of spiders' legs. A mass of these
single flowers cascading from a basket
is a dramatic sight, especially in such a
rich colour. 'Red Spider' is clearly free-
flowering and has long trailing stems.

A suffusion of different pinks makes up 'Merry Mary'. Her bushy frills of white to palest pink look just like a hooped skirt and the long stigma protrudes boldly beneath this colourful attire. The tube and sepals are more of a delicate pink, even more so on the underside of the petals. 'Merry Mary' is a vigorous, free-flowering plant with a natural disposition as a trailer and therefore pre-eminently suitable as a subject in a hanging basket.

'Display' AGM (above) was first described in 1881 and lives up to its name, providing a colourful display not only in a hanging basket, but as a bush or standard specimen as well. It is a free-flowering, hardy plant with single flowers; its oval leaves are very slightly serrated. The vibrant pinks and the elegant way that the sepals are reflexed uniformly upwards make 'Display' a truly distinctive variety.

'Tinkerbell' (left) is a smart-looking fuchsia with fine, clipped features. Its appears mostly white, but the unopened sepals are tinged with green at the tips before they open out with a dusting of pink on the reflexed underside. 'Tinkerbell' does well in baskets – it is compact and flowers freely, contributing vitality and brightness to a hanging basket in a small space.

Highly suitable as a subject in a basket, the double-flowered 'Kathy Louise' (above and right) was first raised in 1963. Its principal attraction is the ruffle of pale pink petals out of which the reproductive parts protrude like a dancer's legs. Above the petals the sepals reflex strongly and have a sort of crêpe effect on their undersides.

Of the many virtues of fuchsias, their prolific flowers are the prime attraction. Some varieties, however, can be inclined to legginess, so a leafy, well-clothed type, such as 'Margaret' AGM (opposite) is especially important in an all-fuchsia basket.

Suspended to encourage even growth all round, a fuchsia basket will make a richly coloured focal point. The added height provided by this ornamental bracket (above) also shows off the individual flowers to best advantage.

The essence of summer: the deep pinks and purples of a frilly fuchsia tone beautifully with royal purple lobelia and the large heads of candy pink pelargoniums in an overflowing mixed basket, one of many adding interest at eye-level in this typically English garden.

It must be the deep purple coloration that gives 'Voodoo' its dark and sinister name – with colours like this, 'Voodoo' is in a class of its own. The flowers, with glossy red sepals reflexed boldly upwards like angels' wings, are freely produced. The fully double skirt is rich pink to deep purple at the edges and the female part of the flower is especially prominent.

Begonias are another traditionally important feature of hanging baskets. There are many types to choose from but perhaps the best and most showy are those called tuberous begonias (*Begonia* x *tuberhybrida*) which typically have very large blossoms and exciting colours.

Begonias are native to the tropics and sub-tropics and are attractive not only because of their stunning colours but also their foliage. The leaves are highly variable, some like small shiny coins, others large and covered in fine hairs or pointed with wavy edges; many have fascinating patterning and spotting. There are at least 2000 species so far known and well over 10,000 named varieties and cultivars. The flowers are borne loosely on slender stalks and vary from white and yellow through orange and pink to magenta and reds. The double nature of some tuberous begonias makes them especially impressive. Although some begonias grow too tall and woody for baskets, there are plenty of small varieties, and compact new cultivars which make ideal subjects. These include the Ornament series, the Clips series and the Memory series, which have large flowers in comparison to the relatively small leaves. Interesting trailing varieties include the white *Begonia solananthera* AGM and *Begonia radicans* AGM with bright red flowers.

Begonias are very versatile plants. They can be grown inside as house plants as well as in conservatories or outside, flourishing in part shade with ample humidity. In a large collection it is possible to have begonias in flower all year round, but the usual way to treat tuberous types is to keep them dormant through the winter. Newly sprouted in spring, the small plants can be transferred to baskets to produce a prolific display well into the autumn.

An enormous sunburst of a begonia making a marvellous display with blue bush violets (*Browallia speciosa*).

The simple colours of this tuberous begonia makes an effective basket. The glowing red-orange contrasts well with the glossy green foliage, punctuated with the orange stamens.

The begonia family is a very varied one. 'Jeanne', for instance, has attractive pink and white flowers, but it is the mound of long wavy leaves that are its chief feature. Planting in a basket draws attention to their bristly red-veined undersides.

'Cherry Blossom' is an interesting double form of the more usual wax begonia (*Begonia semperflorens*). An attractive feature is the way the flowers change from red through pink to white, mimicking exactly the manner in which blossom goes through colour changes from bud stage to open flower. This cultivar would be worth having just because it differs from the all too frequently used regular form. Other new cultivars of this form of begonia include the Olympia series AGM, the Victory series and the Party series.

This tuberous begonia makes a stunning display. The double flowers are large with a very open structure, the petals being rounded and a little serrated around their outer margins.

Begonias and bush violets (*Browallia speciosa*) make excellent companions. In this fine planting, opposite, the stunning red begonia is beautifully complemented by the purple of the bush violets peeping round at the side. A yellow tuberous begonia completes the picture.

The distinctive colour of the flowers of *Begonia sutherlandii* AGM (left), flow prolifically from the mass of large leaves, making this a covetable addition to any garden. This species is a tuberous kind of begonia from Natal in South Africa. It exists in large- and small-leaved forms, both of which typically have the deep lobing at the base of the leaves. *B. sutherlandii* AGM brings an interesting tone to a mixed basket but makes an eye-catching solo act.

Partnering the soft green and orange of *Begonia sutherlandii* AGM with the downy stems of *Helichrysum petiolare* 'Limelight' (left) has brought out their subtle colours. Both are vigorous plants and so one is unlikely to swamp the other. Helichrysums are a justly popular choice for baskets. They keep their attractive foliage for a long time, well into the first frosts. Grown in baskets, they are half-hardy and may grow even bigger in their second year.

Tuberous begonias have been used with their daintier cousins, wax begonias (*B. semperflorens*), together with impatiens and petunias, to plant up this suspended basket made of mossy branches (right). It is a planting ideal for a cooler climate, and the twists of ivy and a hardy fern act as a necessary foil for the bright colours.

FOLIAGE AND FERNS

Foliage in baskets helps to soften a planting, to give it substance and also bring harmony to a brightly coloured mix. But the potential of foliage as a feature in its own right is often underestimated. Baskets planted primarily with foliage plants can remain attractive all year and many plants not grown for their flowers require less light, which increases the possible positions for a basket to hang.

Some of the best foliage effects for hanging baskets are evergreens. There is a number of different plant groups which can be used to make good year-round foliage displays and these include ferns, ivies, vincas (periwinkles) and sedums. Some, such as sedums and vincas, may show off small attractive flowers during some periods of the year, but overall their attraction is their evergreen nature.

The varying texture and forms of growth of leaves can also be impelling virtues in foliage plants. Take into consideration the roughness or glossiness, colour variations and size of leaves when making up a basket, as well as the upright, branching or weeping habit of the whole plant.

Cascades of ivy rain down from this basket which is festooned at the top with a colourful array of *Streptocarpella* flowers.

An interesting study in leaf forms: in this large moss-lined basket stiff, vertical spikes contrast with glossy new leaves (in this case a young camellia) and the sinuous stems of a periwinkle or vinca. Periwinkles make superb subjects in hanging baskets for several reasons. In the wild their far-reaching stems scramble through other plants, which makes them natural trailers when grown in a basket. They live in and under hedgerows and are quite used to regimes of low light, and being evergreen they provide year-round colour. As a bonus, their long stems are punctuated in late spring with small, delicate flowers. These are most commonly purple or blue but there are white varieties and also double forms, and flowers with pointed petals. Under cultivation there are also forms which are grown simply for the attractiveness of their leafy stems and which rarely flower. The variety used here is *Vinca major* 'Variegata' AGM; the silver edging to the leaves provides a lightness which brings out the richness of the other greens and highlights the occasional scarlet impatiens. The only bad news about vincas is that they are poisonous!

The common name for the large leathery bergenia is, appropriately, elephant's ears. It takes on a dominant position in this basket, but then there are few other evergreen plants which can match it for size of leaf and hardiness. The pink or red flowers that the bergenia produces will add a seasonal splash of colour in spring, but it is the contrast of the bold 'ears' with the variegated periwinkle (*Vinca major* 'Variegata' AGM) and plume-like asparagus fern (*Asparagus densiflorus* 'Myers' AGM) which makes this vivid collection of greens a success.

The weeping fig, *Ficus benjamina* (above), is such a common subject as a house plant, often reaching considerable heights, that its use in a hanging basket can be overlooked. Certainly it is not often used in baskets, but here is it well displayed with pink and red impatiens. This, the variegated form, could actually be confused at a distance with a variegated form of bougainvillea (see page 115). To keep the weeping fig within practical limits it must be pruned to shape, and encouraged to weep rather than to bolt upwards. As an evergreen it keeps up a spectacular display throughout the year, only needing to be revitalized by the addition of some simple seasonal accompaniments.

Succulents such as crassulas, sedums and kalanchoes, like this *Kalanchoe pumila* (left), make exciting displays in hanging baskets not least because their firm and juicy foliage comes in a variety of greys, greens and blues. Their tough leaves are remarkably resilient to damage and, as they are expert at conserving water, they will tolerate a certain amount of lack of watering.

It is not hard to see how the coloured flame nettle (*Coleus blumei*) got its name. Leaf patterns come in an amazing combination of jazzy hues such as emerald with a scarlet tongue, magenta and chocolate, and dark green with a bright pink ruffle. A packet of mixed seed always contains a rewarding surprise. The velvety gold-margined variety on the left is teamed up with a plainer relation, *Plectranthus*. Although not as vivid as its cousin, the neat scalloped leaves on trailing stems make the *Plectranthus* an attractive and useful basket plant. *Plectranthus forsteri* (syn. *P. coleoides*) 'Marginatus', above, is a vigorous and trailing variety, with a smart silver edge.

Both *Coleus* and *Plectranthus* are natives of the tropics and will thrive in a good deal of heat. A basket of these would be happy outside for the summer but would need to be brought under cover in cooler weather.

It needs a second look to realize that this, too, is a *Coleus*. Usually it is the leaves that are most notable, but here the flowers grab all the attention. *Coleus* are most usually grown as house plants or perhaps bedded out in summer, but they can be accustomed to life in a basket and in this case a *Coleus* has rewarded the grower with a profusion of flower spikes that have sky-rocketed dramatically. This spectacular effect has, however, been at the expense of the leaves, which have been drained of much of their colour while the plant put its efforts into flower production.

True to its common name, the foliage flower or snowbush (this is *Breynia disticha* 'Rosea Picta', right and below) presents a fascinating colour combination of pink stems and creamy white leaves, not widely seen in other plants. The species is bluish but there are cultivars which have purple leaves, or leaves blotched with red and pink. This plant is a member of the spurge family, the Euphorbiaceae. It sometimes goes by the alternative name of *Phyllanthus nivosus*, and its unusual coloration makes it a very useful plant in garden design. Here it is growing with a little starry-flowered campanula. *Breynias* do well in either full sun or partial shade and can be propagated from cuttings taken straight from the main stems or from the roots.

A plentiful supply of herbs at eye level is not only a tantalizing feast for the eyes but an *aide-mémoire* for things culinary. To be able to pick a posit of parsley or a sprig of thyme close to the kitchen is appealing, and although the idea of growing food in baskets is a relatively new one, it is one which easily excites the imagination. The challenge to grow 'edible' hanging baskets has attracted the attention of many gardeners, who raise not only herbs, but tomatoes, peppers and selected varieties of other produce in conveniently situated baskets.

Young parsley plants introduced to a new basket will flourish with such exuberance that you will find your cooking will not be able to keep up with its leaf production. It is worth experimenting with different types of parsley as it is available in a variety of textures and forms.

To keep all herbs producing succulent young shoots for picking they need to be regularly watered, fed and picked.

Lovage (*Levisticum officinale*), left, flourishes furiously in a green ball, its aromatic astringency encouraging you to sample its leaves.

The fuzzy foliage of thyme, *Thymus vulgaris*, burgeons from this basket (right). To have a ball of thyme hanging near the kitchen is a great bonus for cooking; in the wild, thyme is fairly drought-tolerant and grows on tough little woody stems but frequent picking will keep it tender.

Growing peppers in baskets is fun. At eye level you can inspect the progress from the small white flowers to the large peppers as they mature. The plants have to be inserted into the basket when young and then allowed to grow on. A moss ball is necessary as a sponge to keep the water where it is needed, but after that warmth from the sun is the most important factor.

Ivies (*Hedera* spp.) are the backbone of many hanging baskets, but the several hundred varieties and cultivars include many which deserve a role centre stage. Some of the prettiest ivies for hanging baskets are those with silvery or silver-variegated leaves, which are especially effective in evening light. Below, a silver-leaved variety brings an ethereal glow to a shaded courtyard and the trailing stems fall right into the red leaves of caladiums.

The sedum opposite is about as spectacular as they come. The huge trailing branches are smothered in succulent leaves which overall give the impression of a giant tail or lengths of twisted rope – unsurprisingly its common names include burro-tail, donkey's tail and lamb's tail. The Latin name for this magnficent species is *Sedum morganianum* AGM. As a native of Mexico, this plant is ideal for outdoors in warmer climates and indoors in cooler areas. With its naturally trailing habit, it will cascade to about 1 m (3 ft), and although its most dramatic effect is accomplished from its simple foliage, *S. morganianum* AGM does produce pink-purplish flowers in spring. It can be propagated from the leaves.

Ferns have a fascination in form and detail unrivalled in the botanical world. Some look like delicate filigree, while others, such as the appropriately named ladder ferns, have long fronds which look like a series of steps. In contrast, the striking stag's horn ferns are stiff and broad, just like green antlers. Ferns range through all shades of green, from a delicate lime to dark khaki, and most have the great advantage of looking attractive all year round.

A look at how ferns grow in the wild gives some idea of how suited they are to life in and around the home. The natural habitat for most ferns is in the understorey beneath large trees; some epiphytic types actually grow on the trees' branches, their filmy fronds dangling high above the forest floor. They derive some nutrients through their roots, and some through the green chlorophyll in their fronds, but do not require much feeding or a great deal of root space. Most need only dappled light, but a few ferns live in more open exposed situations. Those that live on the sides of cliffs or in the branches of trees have a natural tendency to cascade which makes them particularly well adapted to baskets. Most ferns featured in this chapter come from the warmer parts of the world and so grow best in a conservatory in temperate climates, moving outside to a shady spot for the summer. They are ideal for those dark corners under cover, adding greenery where few other plants will grow. When planting up ferns, choose a peat-based soil mixture for good drainage and spray regularly to main a high humidity around the plants.

This spectacular mother fern, *Asplenium bulbiferum* AGM, is also called hen-and-chicken fern and king-and-queen fern after the manner in which small reproductive bulblets or plantlets grow on the upper surface of the fronds. Each can become a new plant. The much-divided fronds are also reminiscent of parsley which accounts for its other name of parsley fern. This *Asplenium* is native to New Zealand, Australia and India.

Sword ferns, such as this *Nephrolepis exaltata*, are ideal in shady areas. There are about thirty species of sword ferns, and they are native to the tropical and sub-tropical forests of South America and Asia, so will need the protection of a greenhouse or conservatory. There are over fifty cultivars and varieties of *N. exaltata*: this one is 'Can-Can'. Its distinguishing feature is the way in which the ends of the fronds are heavily divided into clumps of smaller fronds, giving it a frilly appearance.

Two stag's horn ferns (right) embrace their basket to produce a very pleasing symmetry as their broad divided fronds reach upwards and outwards, seeking the light which gives them energy. These are *Platycerium superbum* (= *grande*), and the large enveloping fronds round the basket show a high degree of vitality and healthiness typical of plants growing in optimum conditions. From below one can appreciate the green or brown scaly fronds which make these ferns so attractive, especially when they catch the sunlight and take on a silvery sheen. These fronds are also called 'nest leaves' since they have a tendency to overlap each other, and in doing so accumulate debris. This debris helps to retain water, rather like the effect of mulching, and allows the plant access to water during periods of drought.

Stag's horn (or elk's horn) ferns look weird and wonderful, but are not everyone's first choice. They must be grown in a hanging basket or from a suspended log (see page 25) and enjoy dappled sunlight. Given the right conditions they can make impressive conservatory plants, reaching great age and proportions. In hotter climates they can be grown outdoors but must be given some shade.

Platycerium bifurcatum (= *alcicorne*) AGM (right) differs from *P. superbum* (= *grande*) in having relatively thin fronds which are divided and elegant in form. The new frond growth on the base can be distinguished from the old brown fronds on the basket. Two or three of these ferns make a spectacular display on any basket, but you need space to show them off. These stag's horns are not planted in the basket, but secured to the outside.

These long fronds (left) belong to a major fern, one of the *Davallia* group of ferns native to the forests of south-east Asia. This example is a cultivar of *D. fejeenis* named 'Plumosa', which describes the feathery nature of the fronds. It is epiphytic, occuring on rock, often in exposed situations. It has a unique way of overcoming drought, by using a special joint where the frond meets the rhizome to shed some fronds.

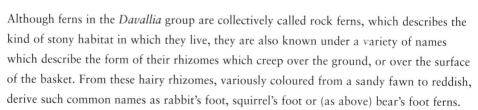

Although ferns in the *Davallia* group are collectively called rock ferns, which describes the kind of stony habitat in which they live, they are also known under a variety of names which describe the form of their rhizomes which creep over the ground, or over the surface of the basket. From these hairy rhizomes, variously coloured from a sandy fawn to reddish, derive such common names as rabbit's foot, squirrel's foot or (as above) bear's foot ferns.

A ferny-orientated arrangement combines the relatively small squirrel's foot fern or ball fern, *Davallia trichomanoides*, with impatiens and fuchsias. It is a compact fern which produces fronds up to 30 cm (1 ft) long and is more tolerant of lack of water than other ferns. Ideally suited to hanging baskets, it does not grow too big and can be mixed with other species. Its home is the rainforests of the Malay archipelago, but little of its native habitat remains today.

The polypody ferns (*Polypodium* spp.) are widely distributed in the tropics, with some in cooler climates. Many suit hanging baskets because of their cascading nature; being suspended also shows off the way that the fronds of many types are subdivided. This one, above, with its fresh green frilly fronds, is *Polypodium* 'Kuddie'. This is a particularly large specimen, but there are plenty of other polypodiums which are much smaller and more delicate. Polypodiums tend to be clump forming and their fronds typically arise from rhizomes. Those of *P. aureum*, which may be up to 1.5 m (5 ft) long, are covered with scales, giving rise to its common name of hare's foot fern.

Asparagus fern (right) is not a true fern, but a member of the lily family, like the edible asparagus, although this one, *Asparagus densiflorus* 'Sprengeri' AGM, is an ornamental species only. However, it is one of the most widely used 'ferns' in the house and makes an attractive addition to hanging baskets, where its fronds can grow up to 2 m (6 ft) long. The asparagus fern is a versatile species that can be used as a climber as well as a trailing plant in a basket; against a trellis it will use its hooked spines for climbing. The foliage of the asparagus fern varies according to where it is placed with regard to the sun: in full sunlight it tends to become lighter than if it is in partial shade.

There are about thirty species of *Nephrolepis* worldwide under various different names, such as ladder fern, Duff's fern and basket fern; all are native either to the tropical Americas or to south-east Asia. *Nephrolepis exaltata*, the sword fern, comes from tropical South and Central America, and is known in perhaps fifty different varieties. One of these, the Boston fern (*Nephrolepis exaltata* 'Bostoniensis') has a more graceful drooping nature than many of its relations and so is much used for hanging baskets. Sword ferns do well in shady areas and in areas of poor light where few other plants, except perhaps ivies, will survive. They do like high humidity,

but can tolerate a certain degree of neglect and irregular watering, a useful attribute. They are fairly hardy but will not tolerate hard frosts. Sword ferns naturally grow in the ground, rather than being epiphytic (i.e. growing on the branches of trees) and reproduce by sending out runners from crowns which will produce new plants. To make more plants, just divide the crowns.

The selection of hanging baskets opposite, with a Boston fern (*Asparagus densiflorus*), an asparagus fern and a spider plant (*Chlorophytum comosum*) lends an air of lush, green calm to this New Orleans courtyard. Their arching fronds reach down to link visually with the pots of impatiens, caladiums and yucca below that thrive in the mild climate.

TROPICALS AND SUB-TROPICALS

For gardeners in temperate and cooler climates, the exotic conjures up the lush growth of tropical rainforests, enormous blooms in startling electric colours and musky scents. The tropics have long been a rich source of house plants – bromeliads, *Coleus* and the ubiquitous rubber plant (*Ficus elastica*) are all natives of tropical regions, and it is but a small step to use these plants and others to create a jungly micro-habitat in a basket.

The brightest parts of tropical plants are not always the flowers themselves. Some plants have insignificant flowers, but have evolved highly decorative leaves or bracts, which serve as a beacon to pollinating insects but distract feeders away from the vulnerable flowers. Other plants have developed a deception technique which also happens to enhance their appeal to gardeners: by making their new leaves and tips a different colour, these vulnerable growths appear not to be part of the main plant, so predators and egg-laying insects move on to find another host and delicate growing shoots are left uneaten.

The stylish *Brugmansia* (syn. *Datura*) popularly known as angel's trumpets.

The vigour of some tropical species can be daunting, but this makes for a bigger and better display. Tough foliage is a reflection of their way of surviving grazing animals and a harsh climate, and that toughness makes them good, stout plants for the house or conservatory. Another virtue of many tropicals is one we have seen already in ferns, that of an epiphytic existence on the branches and trunks of trees. Their light requirement is low and their root systems are relatively small, just sufficient to hang on, so they are naturally predisposed to the restricted life in a hanging basket.

Between the hot wet tropics and the cool temperate zones are the sub-tropics. These touch on the southernmost tip of Florida, but even in the west of Ireland and south-west of Britain the tempering effect of the North Atlantic drift enables many sub-tropical species to thrive. With a conservatory, anyone can create a sub-tropical environment and enjoy the many glorious and unusual plants illustrated in this chapter.

The large strap-like smooth leaves and impressive flowering spikes of this flaming sword *Vriesea carinata* make this a dominant plant to use in any hanging basket display. It is a bromeliad, with long-lasting flowers, a typical epiphytic species of the tropical rainforest of Central and South America. There are at least ten hybrids which have been produced in cultivation, including the painted feather, *Vriesea × mariae*.

Typical of many of its family, the thick leaves of this bromeliad are arranged as a rosette, forming a 'tank' or 'reservoir' of water. As this bromeliad is an epiphytic plant it does not have any substantial main roots from which to feed it, so it puts little roots arising from the leaf bases into the collected water to drink. In the wild the plant collects rainwater in its tank, and up to 5 litres (1 gallon) have been found in one plant. Naturally the tank also accumulates debris, creating a mini-habitat for small aquatic plants and is also frequented by frogs. The centre of the plant needs to be kept full of water.

The pink quill, *Tillandsia cyanea*, from Ecuador is a beautiful bromeliad which makes a great display in a hanging basket. It has a close relative, the blue-flowered torch, *T. lindenii* AGM, but there are many others to choose from. The familiar Spanish moss which festoons trees in the hot and humid south-east of the USA is also a type of tillandsia (*T. usneoides*) and can be used to decorate baskets. The actual flowers of this pink quill are very small and fleeting, but the brilliant flower spike holds its colour for a long time.

Typical of bromeliads, this orange star or scarlet star, *Guzmania* 'Orangeade', produces a vibrant-coloured spike. This inflorescence grows out of the centre of the rosette of leaves and makes a superb specimen as a centrepiece in a hanging basket. The close relationship to pineapples, which also belong to the bromeliad family, can be seen in the tall central spike.

A bromeliad basket brimming full with blooms makes a tropical attraction only if you have the climate to display it. The great thing about bromeliads is that their highly coloured leaves are an asset even when the long-lasting flower spikes eventually fade. The colours are strident and typical of the environment from which they mostly come, the rainforests of tropical America. In nature they live on the branches and trunks of trees and typically take in food and water through their leaves and do not have a large root system for absorption. With over 2000 bromeliad species recorded there are plenty to choose from in garden centres. They enjoy heat and plenty of moisture and may be kept outside in hot climates so long as they are sprayed regularly; in cooler climates they will need a humid conservatory. In this basket are four bromeliads: the magenta *Tillandsia cyanea*, two tall *Guzmania* 'Orangeade', one each side of the centre, and the open flowers of a species bromeliad. Ivy fills the gaps.

The goldfish plant (*Columnea* sp.) is named after the long fish-like flowers which burst from the downy foliage. From the tropical forests of South America, these make superb and vivid hanging basket subjects since in the wild, where there are over a hundred species known, they all have the habit of hanging on to branches and tree trunks in much the same fashion as they are required to cling on to a basket. The pendulous stems on which the flowers are borne can be up to 2 m (6 ft) long and the flowers themselves are generally in bright shades of red, orange and yellow as an attraction to pollinating insects and humming birds.

The goldfish plant will quickly succumb to frost, and so is most suited to a basket indoors or in a conservatory.

Bougainvilleas provide
a wonderful cascade of
colour, but a single frost
will kill them, so they
will need a winter home
in a conservatory.

Bougainvillea 'Raspberry Ice' (above) has variegated foliage which makes it highly distinctive. Slightly lighter in colour is *B.* 'James Walker' (left). Given time and optimum conditions, both these young specimens will grow to the size of the *B.* 'Multicolor', top left.

South African gazanias (*Gazania × hybrida*) add an excellent quality of glowing yellows and oranges to a hanging basket but they do need full sun before their flowers will open. By nature they will sprawl all over the place, but to make an attractive basket they need to be cut regularly so that some of the longer stems take on a trailing habit.

The mask flower (*Alonsoa warscewiczii* AGM) from Peru (below) is not commonly used in a hanging basket, but here it makes a wonderful display with a pelargonium that matches it for colour and a variegated periwinkle (*Vinca* sp.). The brilliant flowers of this annual vary from red to orange and when in full bloom like this the effect is breathtaking. There is a compact form available.

The ubiquitous poinsettia makes a spectacular focal point when displayed in a hanging basket. Poinsettias are most noted for the Christmas market and they get their vivid character not from the flowers, which are insignificant, but from the large coloured bracts which surround the flowers. They belong to the spurge family (with the Latin name of *Euphorbia pulcherrima*) and exist in a number of forms including doubles. Paler varieties last a long time, from Christmas to Easter. The key to success with poinsettias is light control: they produce their bright bracts only when then have experienced a minimum of fourteen hours every day in the dark during the winter period, a thing which is difficult to do at home but necessary to bring back the astonishing colours of the plant for a second year. Poinsettias are conservatory or house plants, but may be kept outside in a basket on a veranda in warmer climates.

This stunning item for the hanging basket (right) is a twining perennial native of tropical Africa – its name is the orange clock vine (*Thunbergia gregori*). It is vigorous and rampant, and in a basket may have to be restrained by judicious pruning, since if planted out it will grow as a vine to 2 m (6 ft). The large flowers are magnificent and with feeding it can be encouraged to bloom all year. Easily grown from seed, this thunbergia is a big and colourful addition to the garden.

The blue trumpet vine, *Thunbergia grandiflora* AGM (above left), certainly has grand flowers that are borne on its climbing and trailing stems. It is woody, evergreen and perennial, and a real treat to liven up a conservatory.

A more familiar thunbergia is black-eyed Susan (*T. alata*), left. It is also a perennial, but is most often treated as a fast-growing annual. Its small, black-centred flowers are frequently seen trained up poles in greenhouses or forming wigwams in tubs, but it also makes a rewarding cascade from a hanging basket.

Yesterday-today-and-tomorrow plant (right) is just one
of the names for *Brunfelsia pauciflora calycina* AGM, an
evergreen shrub from the Brazilian forest; it is also
called the Franciscan nightshade and the franciscea. The
round, sculptured flowers look like those of the potato
family to which it belongs and the glossy pointed leaves
are typical of the genus. Grown in a basket, the plant
has to be restrained somewhat by pruning since it is
vigorous. The flowers are scented, change to blue then
white with age (which explains the first of its common
names), and stay in flower for a long period. It prefers
shady areas rather than full sunshine. Highly typical of
hot Mediterranean-type or sub-tropical areas, this plant
can always be relied upon to bring a strong blue to any
colour scheme.

A well-grown *Streptocarpella* (below) looks superb in
a hanging basket. The lip-like flowers have a striking
colour which is hardly matched by any other plant
likely to be grown in a basket.

One of the great virtues of mandevillas (*Mandevilla sanderi* or *M. dipladenia*) is that they have large, long-lasting, vibrant flowers accompanied by rich green foliage. Whether by themselves or in a mixed planting they will always attract attention. Mandevillas come in a medley of rich colours: on the left is the brightest red, 'Scarlet Pimpernel'; the one above is 'Red Riding Hood'.

Mandevillas reward a little cosseting: give them a rich but well-drained soil and feed regularly throughout the summer flowering season. Overwintered in a frost-free place, they should survive to give an even more gorgeous display the following year.

The large leaves in this basket are those of the dumb cane, *Dieffenbachia* 'Perfecta Compacta'. It is called the dumb cane since the poisonous sap can burn the throat and vocal cords. With its lemon-green variegated leaves, a dumb cane makes an interesting statement in any display. The plant is noted only for its leaves, its flowers being insignificant, and older plants are better to use since they have more than one stem. Mixed here with impatiens in a variety of shades, the dumb cane needs no other accompaniment.

A simple yet spectacular contrast of colour and form is the key to the exotic arrangement on the right. The anthurium (*Anthurium scherzerianum*), bird's nest fern (*Asplenium nidus* AGM) and ivy (*Hedera helix*) will prosper in the warm shade of a conservatory or, in more clement climates, outdoors with protection from the sun. The ever-accommodating ivy will grow in a wide range of conditions, and the bird's nest fern, given shade and sufficient humidity, will grow on to much greater dimensions if given the space. Set against these and against its own plain leaves are the bright spathes which give this flashy anthurium its ornithological common name of flamingo flower.

ACKNOWLEDGEMENTS

The author would like to thank the following for their permissions to take photographs: Neil Odenwald of Baton Rouge, Louisiana; Ric and Ted Mayeda of M & M's Nursery in Orange, Orange County, southern California; Rogers Garden and Nursery in Corona del Mar, southern California; Mrs Evelyn Weidner of Weidner's Nursery in Encinitas, near San Diego, southern California (who has introduced several new plants to the USA); Wade Roberts at the Sherman Gardens, Corona del Mar, southern California; other photographs were taken on Sea Island, Georgia, the Riviera and in the UK. The author would also like to thank Bill and Dee Jasper of Tehachapi and Ed and Mary Fry of Rose Tree Cottage, Pasadena for facilitating matters during my trips to California.

INDEX